THE LIFE SENTENCE OF A SIX-YEAR-OLD

THE LIFE SENTENCE OF A SIX-YEAR-OLD

BY
STEVE LOGAN

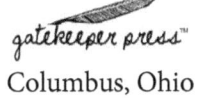
Columbus, Ohio

The Life Sentence of a Six-Year-Old

Published by Gatekeeper Press
2167 Stringtown Rd, Suite 109
Columbus, OH 43123-2989
www.GatekeeperPress.com

Copyright © 2021 by Steve Logan
All rights reserved. Neither this book, nor any parts within it may be sold or reproduced in any form or by any electronic or mechanical means, including information storage and retrieval systems, without permission in writing from the author. The only exception is by a reviewer, who may quote short excerpts in a review.

Library of Congress Control Number: 2021952815

ISBN (paperback): 9781662923180
eISBN: 9781662921285

DEDICATION

*To Alice, Debbie, Robert, Kathy, and Christy...
with my sincerest apologies.*

FOREWORD

"To parents everywhere. Sure, discipline your children reasonably. But love them…without reason."

Late in my life, for reasons still unknown to me, I had a realization. You can call it seeing the light or a calling from God, but I became suddenly, painfully aware of my past and what I had done—or perhaps, I should say, what I had failed to do. Never before had I acknowledged or considered my actions and the painful consequences they brought to others.

When this revelation hit me, it was beyond depressing. And it snowballed. It was not a passing thought either. It stayed with me constantly until I began to realize I didn't like myself. And, as if that wasn't enough, I discovered I couldn't even remember a lot of what I had wrongly done during my failed marriages or shortly after. To me, that meant only one thing: it was worse than I knew.

My conscience was relentless in its occupation of my mind's time. My feelings and thoughts ran the gamut from regret to fear to sorrow and shame. I hadn't had contact with either of my exes or my three kids for forty years.

I knew I had to do something. I wanted to do something. Even if it was met with criticism and scorn. Any rejection would be a normal response to the rejection I had shown them. There were only two possible paths to choose from. One, to contact both exes and kids, not knowing, of course, how that would be received. Or two, to leave things the way they were and had been for the last forty years. This, naturally, meant living out of the balance of my life, thinking about the cold shadow of abandonment I had cast over them.

It was a no-brainer! I knew what had to be done. So I contacted my attorney and explained everything. I made clear that I wasn't looking for an avenue for a solution or to make excuses…just understanding. They were going to learn things about me that neither they, nor anyone else, for that matter, knew of my life. Their response, whether positive or negative, I would accept. And they would be right, because I was at fault. Regardless, I wanted them to have the benefits of my Will. So, I hired a detective who was successful in locating both of my estranged exes and children. Then I sat down and drafted letters to each, explaining my presence and intentions.

To my amazement and gratification, all but one replied positively. I understood the one who rejected my communication. Even so, this was better than I had hoped for or deserved.

I thank them all.

TABLE OF CONTENTS

Foreword vii
Chapter One: The Early Years.. 1
Chapter Two: The Terrible Teens 19
Chapter Three: On My Own 39
Chapter Four: A Life Sentence, Or Closure 45

CHAPTER ONE

THE EARLY YEARS

You better sit down, because what I'm about to tell you won't seem real or possible. It would shock Ozzie and Harriet and most social workers. In 1956, I was a six-year-old who didn't know anything about anybody called "father." Never saw one. Never had one. Hell, I didn't know what one was. Up till I was six, my world was my mother, sister, and grandmother. And they were always busy coming and going. I was like a mannequin that occasionally got hungry.

It was summer, and in a couple of months, I'd be going into first grade. Yet, there were two things I had never heard or known: one, "I love you," and two, my last name! That was about to change.

As a six-year-old, what do you know about life? Love? Family? What you see on TV? What your friends say? How the family next door lives? Of course. Your environment makes more than an impression. It becomes your life, good or bad. And where is an environment most effective? Home. Family. And ultimately, parents! My life was about to change in the summer of '56 with the introduction of this person called "father."

My mother was getting remarried. I never knew my real father. Given Mother's model looks and her Marilyn Monroe likeness, she could have the pick of the litter, the cream of the crop. But apparently, being an attractive blonde precluded her from making good decisions about men. As she would later tell me, this was the worst decision she ever made.

But it was easy to see her attraction. It's often the same as with men. Physical. Six foot, two hundred twenty pounds, and built like the proverbial outhouse. To a scrawny little kid, he was Mr. Atlas. And, as if his daunting appearance wasn't enough, he had a stare that could freeze your body and mind. Instantly, I recognized where I'd seen it before: staring at me through the bars of a lion's cage at the local zoo. His look was as cold and deadly as the lion's stare as it stalked its prey. Projecting death, unemotional, and absolutely fearless. They both showed the same approach to life.

My first introduction to the lion's idea of being a helpful, loving, caring father was learning a last name. It couldn't have been Smith or Jones. That would have been too easy. No, for this frightened little boy of six, learning a last name was a challenge. One made even more daunting by the scornful presence of the lion eyeing my progress. I had a problem getting the letters "au" in the right order. They were in the middle part of my new last name, and, for some odd reason, I was frequently reversing them, much to the lion's displeasure.

The result? I couldn't go to bed until I had correctly written it three hundred times in a row. An error meant starting over! To this day, I can't remember how that story ended, except that he went to bed before me.

It wasn't long before I learned I was more of a tool than a son. Typical of a lion taking over a lioness and her pride, he quickly dispatched her litter. And I considered my fate was just as perilous as any lion cub's. I figured that day had come when we were at a local reservoir used for the city's drinking water and recreational fishing. A physics teacher by trade, he had a summer job there, running the boat rentals.

It was a huge, beautiful reservoir, surrounded by pine trees with many coves as far as you could see. One of those coves appeared in the Gene Hackman movie *Enemy of the State*. When I saw the movie and the familiar spot where the boats were kept, with the short pier that jutted out into the water, I remembered all too vividly my first experience there.

He walked me down the pier and, when we reached the end, threw me into the water. He knew I couldn't swim. No sooner had my head reappeared above the surface than there was another splash. He threw our pet dog in the water too. The dog started to paddle back to shore. The lion roared, "Do what he's doing!" The dog playfully paddled past me, and I knew it was sink or swim. I'd be damned if I'd ever give him the satisfaction of watching me sink.

Suddenly, he dove right over my head and into the water, clothes and all. The sound of car doors closing told him people were coming. Had he changed his mind? Was I "all wet" in my supposition? Then I felt the vise-like clamp of his two hands on my sides, pushing me under the water. Then, just as fast, I was suddenly thrust upward. Instinctively, I grabbed a cross member of the underside of the pier and held on. Just my luck; one of my hands grasped a bee's nest! The stinging began, but I wouldn't let go. That would mean the water again.

Now the bees had found my head. Again, the strength and force of his hands on my shoulders was more than enough to break my grip on the beam. Under I went again, but only briefly. You can't cry underwater. Turns out, swimming wasn't allowed at the reservoir.

Returning home, my hands were red and swollen, dotted with red specks that turned into scars, which remained visible for years. My face, too, was puffy, and my clothes sagging and waterlogged. The lioness was silent when she saw me.

As time went by, my chores increased, and so did the penalties for infractions. It seemed that my sister, two years my senior, was spared from any kind of participation, apparently protected by the lioness. As my resentment grew, I made the mistake of voicing my opinion. Once. The lion replied with a leather belt.

To be honest and fair, I knew all sons probably shared these duties. Mowing the lawn, taking out trash, etc., etc. This I understood. But I also knew daughters in other families had other household chores to do too. There wasn't even any alternating of the most menial of tasks. I mean, how hard and demanding is walking the dog? Yet, many nights, rain or snow, I'd get back at ten o'clock, eleven o'clock, from his walk, and she'd be painting her nails, listening to records, or already asleep! Dishes, groceries; anything and everything fell on me.

The winter of '57–'58 was acutely harsh, setting new record highs for snowfall. During a particularly memorable whiteout blizzard, twenty-eight to thirty inches of snow fell over the span of a day or so. It was unusual for our area. I loved snow! Snowmen, igloos, sledding.

There was, of course, the obvious drawback, and the obvious person to address it. So, with shovel in hand and bundled in my heavy coat and mittens, I'd dig us out. I had to clear the porch, sidewalk, and a flight of steps that led between the house and the street.

There was a silver lining to this cloud. The snow was dry and powdery. It probably took me two to three hours to finish, and when I was finally in, glad to be done, the lion said to me, "Don't take your boots off! Here, go to the store and get a gallon of milk."

Who? Me? Of course, I asked this rhetorically in my mind. What's the matter? She got wet nail polish or something? She could have gone and gotten back before I was even finished shoveling!

The store was only about a mile away and right on our street. By now it was dark. The fifteen- to twenty-mile per hour winds were blowing snow everywhere. Snow removal, street plowing, was, in those days, not a regular or sure thing. Cars were routinely plowed into their parking spaces. However, a plow had recently made a pass, and once I got to the street, the going was easy. I knew then the store would be open, but I was still glad to see the white fluorescent light of the store sign.

The warmth of the store tempted me to dawdle, but I knew I was on the clock, and the lion had zero patience. I was about halfway home when I realized two things. One, it never seemed so cold when I was out playing, and two, a gallon of milk was heavy for a cub.

The next day was beautiful and sunny. And I learned something useful and valuable too. Even as life changed, for better or worse, it stayed with me, maybe too long. It was a way to get out of the house.

I was outside, shoveling the few inches of snow that had blown back over the walk, when three boys, all carrying shovels, walked past. One shouted out, "How much you getting?"

"What?" I answered.

"How much did you get for that?" he repeated.

"Nothing, I live here," I said.

"We get two to three dollars a house!" said one.

"Yeah, and we'll make enough to go to the movies all weekend," said another, "with candy and popcorn too!"

Boastfully, the third boy added, "I got nine dollars already!"

I'd never seen that much money in my young life. Then I realized, too, that money was the currency of escape. With enough of it, I could even morph into a lion. Maybe. The idea was not plausible, but still comforting to an eight-year-old. These neighborhood boys didn't know it, but now they had competition.

My first job was a corner house on the next block with a long walk that wrapped along two whole sides of the property. It hadn't been touched! I don't know how many hours later it was before I finished and knocked on the door. She opened the door and handed me five dollars. Five dollars! I wanted it to snow every day that winter!

I was less than frugal with my newfound wealth. My school was about two miles away, and I usually walked. But for about fifteen cents, I could ride the city bus. I'd walk two or three miles and watch whatever was showing at the Senator Theater. It also meant I could get all the candy I wanted at a drugstore close to school.

I was learning the value and benefits of money. I was dreaming of how I would escape the pride, too young and naïve to know money alone wasn't enough. That was something I would learn the hard way.

I had two friends growing up in the city, Chuckie and David. They were as different as positive and negative. Chuckie lived just down the alley. He was a big kid with a darkness to his skin, tall, big boned, with large hands and feet, but rather clumsy and not athletic at all. David, on the other hand, was more my size. He was very coordinated, the outdoorsy type. He lived a quick mile away by bike. I liked his family. His parents were swell. His sister wasn't bad either! I spent many a weekend at his house. We both were Boy Scouts and often went camping together. One summer, they even took me on their vacation to Rehoboth Beach. I wished I was Dave's brother.

One day after school, while waiting for the bus, Chuck and I got into a fight. I don't know what it was about, but we went rolling around, arms and legs flying everywhere! Chuck was getting the worst of it and began to cry. "It's not fair. You have a father!"

I thought, "You can have mine!" I never knew he didn't have a father. He didn't know it, but he was actually better off without one than I was with mine. The last time I ever saw Chuckie was 1963.

Like a lot of kids, I didn't have perfect teeth. I was even a little bucktoothed. I suppose the lioness expected and wanted me to have a movie star smile like hers. So braces were the order of the day. I must have gotten the bargain basement package. Even though I was a little kid, I knew when something wasn't right. You're not supposed to hear your teeth crack when the bands are tightened around them. But who would have listened to me? The lion? Hell, who'd be dumb enough to complain to the lion? Not me!

Mr. David S., DDS, should have been a medical examiner instead and confined his talents to the dead! Needless to say, I got cavities galore. I needed two molars extracted. I had never gotten a tooth pulled, at least not by a dentist, and of course, the thought of it was scary. It didn't seem to bother the lion or lioness, though.

"You've got a one o'clock dentist appointment. Get your bike, and don't be late," he roared.

I was a really good bike rider, but the front wheel shook all the way there. Pedaling the bike back presented a new problem. The squishing of the blood-soaked cotton in both sides of my mouth made breathing a bit harder. Especially since I knew if I kept my mouth open, the blood would drip down the front of my shirt. Ruining a perfectly good shirt would be one of those infractions worthy of at least a session with the ping-pong paddle. I kept my mouth shut for three miles.

We lived in a small, two-story row house with a finished basement. You could hear the lion roar from the basement to my room on the second floor. As I got older, punishments changed. The days of smashing my hand on the dinner table with some available utensil, a ping-pong paddle, or a belt had passed, replaced by something befitting my age and size. What didn't change, however, was the option of pants up or down. The lion made sure nothing lessened the intended effect. Too many times, the result made it so uncomfortable I couldn't sit on the toilet.

I began to try to prevent myself from going by sitting on my foot to keep from having a bowel movement. A temporary fix that didn't always work and occasionally made for soiled underpants that I would later have to hide. I'd bury them in the trash and then immediately take out the garbage. Sometimes I couldn't get downstairs without being seen, so I'd throw my underpants out the second-story window, then go down, retrieve them, and trash them. The lioness must have wondered what was happening to my underpants. I think she knew the answer was not good.

Up till now, the instruments that delivered punishment had been restricted to the hand, paddle, or belt. One day, that changed. It was a typically hot, humid day. I followed the stretched-out garden hose, carrying a bucket of soapy water and a sponge. At the end was the car, and the lion was spraying it down. I went to the other side, grabbed the sponge, and began washing the sides and windows. Big mistake.

I don't know which arrived first, the sound of his voice or the can of whitewall cleaner. It happened so damn fast! I barely had time to turn my head. It was like a batter getting hit in the face by an errant fastball. I only managed to get my head partially turned so the can impacted my cheek and upper lip. The taste of blood was instant. Then the pain.

"I told you to start at the top, didn't I?" he yelled. The impact tore the inside of my lip across a misaligned and pointy tooth.

I can't remember much after that, except that eating was a challenge. But I still run my tongue over the scar on the inside of my lip to this day, and that is reminder enough. Another lesson and showcase of the lion's strength, speed, agility and temper. And, unfortunately, not for the last time.

1962 left two lasting impressions. The image of one is still, and always will be, fresh in my mind almost sixty years later.

It was around Valentine's Day, February 14, when I got really sick. The doctor said I had tonsillitis, strep throat, and scarlatina (a mild form of scarlet fever) all at the same time. In those days, doctors actually made house calls. The doctor rolled me over and pulled down my pants. I knew what was coming. Or so I thought. Suddenly, WHACK! The palm of his hand hit one cheek while the needle went into the other. Before I had time to appreciate it, he whacked the just-injected side! Another shot followed in the side already decorated with his handprint.

"Sorry about that, but it makes it hurt less," he said.

I thought, *Doctor, you have no idea how painless that was, comparatively.*

I was bedridden for two weeks. I watched as John Glenn rode Friendship 7 into space on my birthday, February 20. All that time, I never saw or heard the lion. I'm not sure I wanted to get better!

My second impression from that summer of 1962 was when the lion crossed the line. The night started like any other. That day and evening had been calm and quiet, with no indication that a volcano would erupt as we slept.

It sounded so loud and close that my first waking reaction was to ball up in a fetal position. The sound of raining pieces of glass in a bucket and the accompanying scream was something to be found only in movies. I waited a few seconds, expecting to feel something hit me. Then, like the aftershock of an earthquake, came the low moaning and crying of a female's voice. There was no mistaking it. It was the sound of the lioness in pain. Somehow, I knew he was responsible. It was very dark, but I made my way toward the sound as fast as I could.

The lion's frame filled the bathroom doorway. The light was on, and I saw my mother's folded-up body. A lot of blood covered her mouth and chin, and her legs were dangling outside the tub. Everything now was strangely silent. I thought he had killed her! I stood frozen in fear of being next.

It had taken only one blow from the lion's fist to send the lioness through the shower's sliding glass doors and into the tub. Lying in bed that night, fearing more to come, but this time my way, I realized something I'd never considered before. Was it possible my mother might have wanted to come to my defense all these years but been held fast by the same fear as I? My guilt for not having thought of this before brought tears to my eyes.

It was then I said to myself, *One day, I'm going to have to kill him...*

The next morning, I knew I had to be careful not to let my face display any sign of my anger. To do so would be tantamount to calling him an asshole. So I called him that over and over in my mind, trying to channel all my anger inward. I then cautiously looked into their bedroom. Mother was alone. Asleep. Even from a distance, you could easily see the large, swollen lip and the evenly spaced dark lines of the stitches. Six, maybe seven.

I don't know how long after that I made my first childish effort to escape. My best friend David and his family had moved outside of the city. They were in a suburb about twenty miles away. I'd been there before. They lived in a big old house with a barn and a pond! I really liked it. With nothing more than a little snow money and the clothes on my back, I headed out. I guess I should be proud that I made it. Sticking to small roads and streets, I walked the entire way without getting lost in about six hours.

It was around midafternoon when Dave's mother opened the door and looked genuinely surprised to see me. She didn't immediately say anything. She was busy looking left and right for whomever had dropped me off. It didn't take long for her to put two and two together.

Later that evening, they showed up to claim their prized son. Now, for the first time since I left, I felt the fear and dread of having to face the consequences of what I had done. Dave already suspected. He whispered, "What's going to happen to you?"

I couldn't tell him. So, nervously, I replied, "Oh, nothing."

I never saw Dave or his family again.

CHAPTER TWO

THE TERRIBLE TEENS

Through all these years and even into high school, fear was the dominant thought I carried constantly in my head. Do you know how hard it is to function normally when that's all you think about? Even the most trivial, menial things were hard to focus on or do. I couldn't concentrate. I didn't know how to relax or allow myself to have fun because I felt there was always something I did or didn't do that was going to result in some form of punishment.

My grades suffered. In grade school, I took the risk of hiding deficiency notices teachers sent home by sliding them under the quarter round molding where the wall met the floor. As I got older, I still went to bed early, pulling the covers over my head in a childish attempt to feel protected. Often I'd leave the light on and books open on the card table used as a desk, to give the appearance I'd been studying. I couldn't even eat my meals without the ever-present fear of the heavy handle end of the silverware knife on the back of my hand, the lion's instant enforcer. Forget dessert. I wanted away from there.

It wasn't long before I realized the safest place to be was anywhere but home. In 1964, we moved to a southern State, to a small town known for its university. I immediately set out to find ways to keep me from having to go home after school. I spent a lot of time at the university's indoor pool and a campus spot called the Tin Can. It was a sports center. I suppose it got its name from the metal siding used as walls. Not exactly what you'd call state of the art.

There was an indoor track, basketball, and something that really interested me: a self-defense class. Some guys were sitting around what looked like mattresses. In the center stood two men in white pajama-looking outfits tied closed at the waist with blue or black belts. I loved it! I could fight back.

One day the instructor said to me, "You've got a gift. The fastest reflexes I've ever seen for kids your age or, for that matter, a lot of adults. I'd like you to come regularly and join." Then he said, "Come here. I want you to try something." He took me over to a chair and got two quarters out of his pants pocket. Holding a quarter in each hand between his index finger and thumb, with his arms straight out in front of him, he dropped them both at the same time. Then he caught both falling quarters in one hand. It was so fast, I almost missed what he did.

I didn't fully realize how hard it was until he explained how it had to be done. The hand used to catch both quarters, about a foot apart and at just about waist height, had to be kept knuckles up toward the ceiling the whole time. No turning the hand over and sweeping across to grab them.

He said, "Try it."

I failed on my first attempt, catching only one. On my third attempt, I caught them both!

"Good! I knew you could do it. Now, try it again, only this time catch the left one first, then the right one."

Being right-handed, I naturally caught the quarter on the right first when I had done it before. The look on my face must have shown him how improbable I thought it was to do.

He said, "Here, let me show you." Brother, that was fast! Needless to say, I was impressed.

This time, I was nervous. I was sure I'd fail and disappoint him. And I did…six times! Sometimes not even getting one! On the seventh try, I held my hand out and opened it. Two quarters!

"Well done!" he said. It was the first time in my life anyone told me I did something well, and it felt good!

So I began to participate in the self-defense classes. I had my own gi and white belt. I learned kicks and punches, even some judo. It wasn't long before the instructor explained to me that my skills were better suited to boxing, as he saw in me a talent for that particular style. This gave me an enormous amount of self-confidence, which I never had before.

This didn't go unnoticed by the lion, who was privy to my boxing efforts. Much to my surprise, he bought two pairs of lightweight boxing gloves so we could occasionally spar in the basement. I'm not sure if he enjoyed hitting me as much as I did hitting him! Of course, it was no real contest, otherwise I probably wouldn't be here now. However, occasionally, he would fall down and pretend to be hurt. After some weeks of sparring, the gloves were split, and I was well educated.

At this time, I also had my own paper route. My twenty-inch bike had a big basket on the front, and I delivered papers to a lot of rural houses, some on dirt roads. One day, on one of those dusty dirt roads, I apparently was careless when throwing the paper onto a porch. The boy who lived there took offense. About my age and a little shorter and stockier, he came running at me, yelling something. I threw my bike down, figuring he was planning on knocking me off it anyway. His angry face reminded me of the lion, and as soon as he was within my reach, my straight left jab landed squarely on his right eye. I didn't hesitate.

His fists and arms came up. I hit him again. And again. And again. He never hit me. He never touched me. He never even got close. I didn't care. It was the lion's face I was pummeling. I must have hit him ten or fifteen times, all left jabs. I didn't know anything about fighting. I didn't know that a good right could end a fight. I had never hit anyone for real before, and I really just wanted to keep him from hitting me.

Finally, half bent over and holding his face, the boy staggered back to the porch in retreat. I finished the route and as I headed home, wondered if I should say anything. An easy decision—NO. I also realized I'd have to go back there tomorrow.

The next day, as I neared that house, I saw the boy and two other taller boys on the porch. One of them pointed at me and said, "*He* did that to you?"

I guess they expected someone bigger! What exactly had I done? I wasn't sure. Then he came down the porch, and I got a closer look at the effects of all those punches in one place, and it damn well scared me. I'd never seen anything remotely like it. The whole right side of his face was a collage of colors. Black, purple, and a sickening yellow.

It almost made me vomit. Any second now, I expected the other two to take their revenge. I'd lose, but I'd hurt at least one of them. I didn't move. And neither did they. Then I pushed my bike forward and pedaled away hard. I didn't waste any time leaving without delivering their paper. It was then that another thought came to mind.

What if that boy's parents told the lion? What if the lion saw the kid's face? Every time the phone rang that night, it made me want to pee my pants. Maybe I should have fessed up about what happened. I didn't sleep much that night.

A few days went by, and I slowly started to unclench. The next time I saw the boy on the porch again, the bruising looked like a shadow cast over one side of his face. I stopped and held out the paper and said, "Here."

He replied, "Okay, just throw it." I found out what I wanted to know. There was not going to be any retaliation by him or his friends.

That fight had a lasting effect on me. I never wanted to fight again. I vowed to avoid fighting whenever possible. I didn't want to hurt anyone like that again. I always hoped that boy didn't suffer any eye damage. With one exception, I was able to keep that promise to myself.

It wasn't long after that we moved back to my home State. Not in the same house and not in the city, but to an older three-story house in the country just north of the city. A new friend, another Dave, lived down the street, and we hung out together. He reminded me of my old friend I grew up with in the city. He was the same outdoorsman type, strong, muscular, but not overly coordinated. He took me shooting with his rifle in the woods. We played basketball in his driveway.

It was during one of those games that I accidentally tore his shirt pocket. I'd never seen him get mad before, but his angry expression and clenched fists got my attention! I figured if he ever got his hands on me, I was a dead duck. No sooner was he within reach than the first of two lefts landed squarely on his nose. It was over that fast.

"I'm a hemophiliac!" he shouted as blood ran from his nose. I didn't know what that meant, but I guessed it had to do with him bleeding. We remain friends to this day!

I came to hate our house, with one interesting exception. My sister and I had bedrooms on the third floor. The lion and lioness were on the second floor, along with the bathroom and a room with a pool table. The first floor was typical, living room, dining room, and kitchen. But in the kitchen there was something very unusual: a door that concealed a hidden staircase that wound its way to the third floor! I immediately saw its value.

The basement was reminiscent of a dungeon. It had low ceilings and exposed pipes, stone walls, and a dampness that was ever present. At one end was half a flight of steps leading outside. It was covered by a hinge "door" that was really a cellar door. Every time I see Dorothy's family take shelter from the tornado in *The Wizard of Oz*, I think of that door.

By now most physical punishment was, with an occasional departure, replaced with mental ones, in the form of restrictions. The possibility of a lightning right or flying object aimed at my face was still ever present, but at times the restrictions were actually worse. The effects were longer lasting and a source of public embarrassment. I'm sure my friends and classmates suspected something was odd when I declined their invitations again and again. The embarrassment of those times often made me prefer the belt.

Before we left our temporary southern residence, the lion had bought a new dog, a shepherd with papers showing he was a distant relative of the original Rin Tin

Tin. It was his dog but my responsibility. The dog listened to him. Smart dog. I knew this because he'd lower his head and ears and put his tail between his legs whenever the lion roared.

I'm not a vet, but the dog did seem to have diarrhea a lot, perhaps on account of his nerves. He'd use the basement as his place of relief, and I needed a snow shovel to even start cleaning up. I think he wanted to get away almost as much as I did. One night, he didn't want to come back from his walk, and when I finally caught him and tried to hook him on the leash, he bit one of my fingers. I made the mistake of telling on him because I thought I might need a doctor.

The following week, the lion and lioness were going away for three or four days, and before they left, he told me, "Take him to the shelter and leave him. I don't want to see him when I get back." Was the lion showing a sign of weakness because he wouldn't or couldn't do it himself? Or was he really as cold and callous as I feared? Then again, was he purposely trying to hurt me by making me do it?

For the first time, I defied him. I figured that by the time he returned, he would have changed his mind. I should have known better. To say he was angry upon seeing his dog still there was putting it mildly. He literally threw us into the car! He grabbed the dog by the scruff of the neck with one hand and held him straight out, five feet off the ground. All eighty pounds of him, like it was nothing. The poor dog yelped and kicked to no avail.

I cried. I felt guilty. My mind was racing through memories of hate I, at times, had toward the dog. The chores that resulted. Late-night walks in all kinds of foul weather. The shoveling of his excrement and washing the soiled concrete basement floor. The disobedience he showed me, and lastly, the bite. But I never wanted him condemned to death.

Later that night, I wept again, and even more now that he was gone. The lion was unemotional, then and later.

As we pulled into the shelter parking lot, the dog became agitated. He knew. Once inside, he fought to keep out of the cage, tearing some of the buttons off the front of my shirt as his paws raked down my chest. So much for the lion's compassionate side. The shelter vet took one look at the lion and made the smartest decision of his life—not to question his motive.

The lion's propensity for physicality wasn't always confined to myself or the privacy of our house. I remember the time he was asked to assist a female teacher to chaperone a school dance at the high school where he taught physics. I'm sure it hadn't escaped the organizers' attention that he would be the last person anyone, student or teacher, would want to start trouble with. He was the obvious choice, and he obviously had an invisible throne in the principal's office! Their faith in his abilities would be tested this night.

As the story went, the female teacher asked a male student to take his cigarette outside, as smoking in the school was prohibited. This kid must not have been aware of the lion's presence, eyeing his every move from across the lobby. Smoking at all was strike one. As the lion keenly watched, the kid went out one door and immediately reentered the lobby through another, cigarette still hanging from his lips. That was strikes two and three. His fate was now sealed. Not only had he flagrantly disregarded the teacher's request, but the lion detested smoking. So the lion, seeing this kid thumbing his nose at the teacher, the rules, and the school, approached him.

Supposedly the kid didn't take kindly to what was probably a distinct roar from the lion and tore the chest pocket of his sport coat. Witnesses said the lion only hit him once, but the force drove him backward about seven feet and into a recessed trophy case with sliding glass doors, shattering them and spilling trophies and glass across the floor. Both he and his cigarette were out.

Naturally, there was a huge fallout. The parents filed a seventy-thousand-dollar lawsuit, the outcome of which I wasn't privy to. Needless to say, the lion taught at a different high school after that. I was not there to witness the incident myself, but I never even considered any part of the event to be exaggerated. After all, I'd seen it once before…

The hardest restriction came in my senior year. I was a sophomore in my first year in my new school. I immediately looked for something to do after school, an excuse to not go home. In the fall of my sophomore and junior years, I went out for the cross-country team and made varsity. As a senior, I tried out for the school's first-ever soccer team and again made varsity. The other schools in the county all had well-established soccer teams, yet we won every game except the championship game, which we lost 1-0. Spring meant track and field season. I made varsity all three years. I found running a joy, a relief.

I recall the first trial mile I ran with another boy, Ed. No sooner had we crossed the finish line, than I got sick! My lunch lay in the grass at my feet. I said to myself, "That's the last mile I'll ever run!"

Wrong! Coach Brown decided I was his miler. I came to admire, respect, and like this man. Coach Brown was a man who was an athlete in his own right. He had claimed the silver medal in the half mile at the Olympics. Not only was he a great coach, but he was a fine man. I still have a letter from him when he turned ninety-three! Sadly, his wife had just died, and, probably unable to live without her, he passed shortly thereafter too.

His legacy will be having coached the greatest high school track team the state ever had! But the best part is, we competed in the toughest division, the "AA" division, and we were the first—and I believe still, the only—school to win back-to-back championships, 1967 and 1968! I had the further honor to be voted in as one of the tri-captains of the '68 team.

If there is one day every senior looks forward to, it is senior cut day. On this day, seniors would cut classes the whole day. My friends kept this tradition, and I joined them. We spent the day in Washington, DC, doing what guys do—going to strip bars and drinking beer! We had a track meeting coming up and didn't have practice that day. Perfect! Well, at least that was the plan. I tried to have as much fun as my friends, but there was one thing holding me back. Their parents knew about cut day and had given them permission to skip class. Mine didn't, and it worried me. But I'd be home on time and sober. Hell, how could they find out, right?

At dinner that night, I got the answer. I knew I was caught as soon as the lion asked, "Where were you today?"

How did he find out? Turns out our school football coach knew the lion! So when he didn't see me in school that day, he called home to see if I was okay. So far I was, but I wouldn't give you odds on it. I figured I might as well confess.

"You're staying home Saturday," he replied. What?! *Over my dead body or yours,* I thought. Saturday was the track meet.

I remember standing in the doorway to their bedroom in the middle of the night. Across my chest, I was holding his .22 caliber rifle. The thought of jail wasn't on my mind. Nor was the thought of the repercussions my mother would face later. Nor the thought of killing him. It was the thought of *not* killing him I was contemplating. Would a .22 caliber bullet be enough to kill a lion? What if I missed? What if I needed a second shot and there was only one bullet in the rifle? I knew I couldn't depend on a torso shot to do the job. It would have to be in the head.

The end of the rifle shook slightly as my nervousness went from my arms to my hands to the trigger. Failure would surely mean the end of me! And that was a risk I just wasn't able to take, a sacrifice I wasn't about to make.

I retreated. Beaten again. As I quietly climbed the stairs to my room, I thought, *It's time to go. Really. Now.*

Here's the strange thing. Sometimes you have to experience something before you believe it. For me, it was sleepwalking. I thought of it only as a comic stunt you see in movies. But then it happened to me. Twice! I was in my forties when it made me a believer. The first time, I got out of bed in the middle of the night, went to the kitchen, opened the silverware drawer, picked up a small steak knife, and placed it in the toaster…plastic handle down. Then, of course, you have to toast it. Which I did. As I waited for the knife to be done, I woke up. Better later than never. But the handle of the knife was already severely melted.

The second and last time I sleepwalked, I wasn't aware of it till the next morning. But when I saw what I had done, I was able to recall doing it! I realized my midnight stroll when I went to make coffee. The empty plastic bottle, which usually held the freeze-dried instant coffee, was lying on its side on the counter, and there was no sign of coffee anywhere. It had been practically full when I made coffee the day before.

Now, I'm not the sharpest tack in the box in the morning before I've had my coffee, so I guess it was just reflex when I started looking for the missing coffee on the counter, on the floor, in the sink…Then it hit me. I had gotten up the night before and made "iced tea." I opened the refrigerator door and took out the pitcher. Mystery solved! The dark liquid that filled the two-quart pitcher wasn't iced tea; it was my missing coffee. And talk about strong!

There's another thing I now believe in. I'd heard that when a person experiences extreme fear or traumatic events, the shock of it can cause them to block it out of their memories. I never put much stock in it. But I'm here to tell you; it's very true! To this day, I have no recollection of what happened after that night. I don't even know if I went to the track meet or not! It's just a blank to me. And believe me, I've tried to fill it in. And then, I come to the realization that I can't recall a lot of things, things that hurt the most.

After barely graduating from high school, I got a job as an iron worker in local 16. And me with acrophobia! But at $6.50 an hour, I gladly faced the fear! It put escape on the horizon. All my life, working weekends during school, I'd never made more than minimum wage, which at that time was $1.25 an hour. My first day, I got up at five in the morning and walked five miles to catch my ride for the twenty-five-mile trip to the construction site at N. Charles and Pleasant Street.

On my way to the site the first morning, I wondered how high the building had already reached. I figured, with my luck, no less than fifty or so stories. Imagine my relief when we pulled up and the steel was only at street level. Phew! Well, almost. Turned out that was the third floor. The building started three stories below ground. Still, learning to walk the iron was made easier by starting at street level.

CHAPTER THREE

ON MY OWN

It was on this first construction job I met a kid who was headed back to Ft. Hood in Killeen, TX, when the job ended. I said to him, "Do you want to save half your gas money?"

He replied, "You're on! Is there another job there?"

"I'll find one!" I answered.

The plan was simple, if it worked. I needed to meet him in town, about a mile from home, at 4:00 a.m. with no more than a small shoulder bag. He drove an MG or MGB, so there wasn't room for luggage. The hard part would be getting out of the house without getting caught. Down the spiral staircase that led to the kitchen and, most importantly, bypassing their rooms on the second floor. Opening and closing the kitchen door leading to the backyard and getting through town on foot, carrying my bag at four in the morning, without some roving, curious cop ending it all!

It wasn't until I saw the kid pulling up that a feeling of freedom raised my adrenaline. This time, I was legal, and I had money. I had finally made it out. It took me twelve years!

Our first stop was Memphis, I think. We hit a hamburger joint and a liquor store, not necessarily in that order, before finding a motel along the main drag. We ate, cleaned up, and took our Thunderbird wine for a ride. It was a beautiful night in an awesome city! We cruised up and down the strip. *So, this is what living is like*, I thought. What I didn't think about was what was happening back home. And I really didn't give a damn.

We pulled back into the motel for the night. For the first time in years, since the summer I was six, I really felt good about going to bed.

The next morning, we were off to an early start. Next stop, Texas. He had friends in Waco, so we stopped there first. They agreed to put me up until I found a job and a place to live. I quickly got work helping to install countertop laminate and carpet in a new apartment development. It wasn't long before I bought an old '53 Chevy. Then I got a new job at a place called Wesson Biscuits. They made cookies, and my job was running a machine that made boxes, much like those that Girl Scout cookies come in.

It was during my lunch break from that that I met Sherry. She worked at a nearby eatery called Twin Kiss, serving their burgers and fries. I often think of her to this day. She was like a little redheaded Farrah Fawcett. We saw a lot of each other, and I knew she wanted us to settle down. It was around this time that I got a place of my own, a mobile home on its last legs in a tiny trailer park. There were six trailers in all, three on each side of a dirt road that ran between them.

I don't know how much time passed since I had left home without a word. And I hadn't heard anything from home in all this time. I never gave it much thought either until…

It was a typically hot, humid Texas day. I had been switched to the graveyard shift at work, midnight to 8:00 a.m. So I was still up when the long black front end of the limo quietly rolled by the door. What the hell? I thought, who'd come here in a limo? Nooo…way! It couldn't be. The rear door opened before the driver could do it. And out stepped the lion! And me without so much as even a baseball bat. The fear was still with me, and now it was walking to my door.

Open the door? Why? He'd probably take care of that. Door lock, doorknob, hinges and all. Much to my amazement, he actually knocked. I could feel his eyes fixed on me. Reminiscent of the past, I froze. A full minute probably passed before I moved and opened the door.

"Your mother's been in the hospital." He said it in the most subdued tone of voice I had ever heard him use. I don't know what he said next. Something along the lines of coming home. He then turned, got back in the limo, and left. I never answered him. Now they both wanted *me* to do something for *them*. And I wasn't sure I would.

I closed the door and sat down to think. I coldly considered my two options and their possible repercussions. It was then that I thought of what might have transpired when I left. I had given my family no warning, no note, nothing. I just disappeared. How big an upset might it have caused? News? Police? A town alert? Had they suspected I was a victim of foul play?

I selfishly thought, *I can get back at him through her.* It was only then that I gave any thought to her. I reasoned that since he was there, they've known my whereabouts for a while; therefore she, too, knew and would be relieved and would get better. Was that just an excuse not to return? Then there was, again, the lion. What would his reaction be if I once again gave him home-field advantage? Thinking back to what he had done to the dog, I had all the information I needed.

I had to get some sleep if I was going to work that night. I awoke a few hours later from a restless sleep, still needing a decision. At work, I mechanically stood at my station, watching a box exit the stamper every couple of seconds. There wasn't anyone I could look to for help or advice, except maybe Sherry. But if she knew too much, it might frighten her or scare her off.

You know, good stories often have good endings, happy endings. But life isn't always like that. You can't always have what you want. Things don't always work out your way. In fact, they rarely do.

What I did will make some of you happy. Others may think I was wrong. You can't please everyone. So I ask you…What would you have done?

CHAPTER FOUR

A LIFE SENTENCE, OR CLOSURE

By now, I was living back in my home state. I lived on my own, and I drove a truck. I met my first wife working at a bar her parents owned. Respectfully, it was definitely a hillbilly joint. And I liked it. She was a barmaid and fixed breakfasts and lunches from a short menu. It wasn't exactly the beer and food that were the main attraction. She was our own Daisy Mae Clampett! The pool table and shuffleboard were busy with blue-collar good ol' boys that stayed busy trying to keep her attention. I was no exception. Why she chose me was a mystery and a pleasant surprise. And I could tell it surprised a few of them too. Did she see me as a pretty city boy?

Anyhow, we started dating. A lot. One night we were particularly late, getting in around 1:00 a.m., and true to movie form, her father met us on the porch. He was sitting on the steps with a shotgun across his lap! I kept that in the back of my mind for future reference! All in all, though, he wasn't a bad guy.

One day he told me I had a job with Raymond-Dravo-Langerfelder if I wanted it. He worked for them, and it was a union job, so the money would be very good. At the time, the job was building the second span of the Chesapeake Bay Bridge. I worked from 6:00 p.m. to 6:00 a.m., and we even got paid for the time it took a boat to get us out to the place we were needed. At the end of our shift, we'd return to the bar for breakfast, beer, and pool!

On one weekend night, as she and I were leaving the bar, we had to walk past a few of her admirers, and one of them whistled at me. This was not the time to show weakness, but I needed to isolate the offender. I went to my car and got out a starter's gun from under the seat. I was gambling on them not knowing the difference from a real one. I fired it in the air and asked, "Who's the one with the sweet lips?"

They all moved...except one! I "convinced" him to follow me into her house, which was right next door. He made the same mistake as the boy who didn't like the way I'd delivered his newspaper, but as I looked at this man, I remembered the boy's bruised face again. So I only changed the pitch of his whistle two or three times. I never had a problem at the bar again.

Sooner or later, I guess it was bound to happen. She got pregnant, and we got married. We were just twenty-one when she had the twins. A boy and a girl. By now I was working for a company that rented TVs to hospital patients. I serviced three hospitals, seven days a week. And meanwhile, she took care of everything. I don't know how she did it. I was no more use to her than the mailman. She deserved better, and anyone else would have been better! I was never home. I was totally inconsiderate, to say the least. And that's putting it mildly. I had a problem.

We separated and divorced. I never saw or heard from them again, not for forty years. I moved around, changed jobs a lot, and still preferred being away from where I lived. I had no contact with anyone in either family. Not Christmas, no birthdays, nothing.

While working for a company called Panelrama, selling wall paneling and kitchen cabinets, I met a waitress at a restaurant called the White Coffee Pot. She was gorgeous! Her statuesque figure immediately caught my attention. I decided to eat breakfast, lunch, and dinner there until she went out with me. I was several years her senior, but apparently that didn't bother her, and we started seeing each other. Had I finally found love? Was this love? How was I to know?

Again, the inevitable happened, I guess. She got pregnant, and we married. We had a daughter, the spitting image of her mother. I made the decision to change jobs for one that paid better. I had a friend whose father sold cars for a living, and he got new cars to drive for free! Then those cars were sold as "demos." I tried to find a job selling cars too. All the big "houses" or dealerships only wanted experienced salesmen, and that's where the bigger money was to be made.

Finally, I got hired at a small dealership in the city, some distance from home. The showroom only had room for four cars! The inventory was stored above, on the second and third floors. Again, the hours were long, and you worked most holidays. A sixty-hour work week was the norm. Physically and mentally, it was demanding. I almost failed. I had been there a month already without selling a single car. The manager was close to firing me when the worm finally turned. That's when I started staying out nights after work.

I could see the pattern starting to repeat itself. She took care of everything again. But to no avail. It was me. I had the problem. The end result was the same, divorce. I had trashed another good woman and family.

It was sometime during the course of these events that another divorce took place. The lion was out! And I missed it! That would have been cause to celebrate, but I was already doing enough of that and still living without an ounce of concern for others. I worked all the damn time! I would only go home just long enough to satisfy my need for sleep. Mentally, I was screwed up, and I didn't even realize it.

I don't know how many relationships I went through. Probably fifteen or twenty. I never allowed any of them to get too close. I figured if you went through enough women, you'd eventually find love. That couldn't be further from the truth. I wasn't looking for love; I was chasing lust. It was only physically satisfying.

I began to think I wasn't the "type" that could ever be in love. Certainly not in love enough to stay with someone for forty or fifty years. It didn't help matters when I found friends, couples who had been in love and married ten, fifteen, twenty years, and I would think, *They're lucky. That's love.* Or, *I need someone like her.* And then it was always a big surprise to everyone, myself included, if one of those perfect couples parted ways. Those divorces put a serious damper on my attitude toward this thing called love. Love. An emotion so powerful it can cement two people together for life…or take a life.

Still, even as the years slipped quickly by, not even my mother was a concern to me. I had no idea what was happening with her. Then something totally unexpected happened. I was asked to meet a man for dinner and a drink. I didn't understand why, but I did. He was short, stocky, and very ordinary in appearance. The complete opposite of the lion. I actually felt comfortable and at ease as we lifted beers. Suddenly, very nonchalantly, he said, "How would you feel about me seeing your mother?"

I'd spent years nervously on guard when questioned. How could this man make me feel so unguarded? I was stunned! Had I heard him correctly? When I recovered from the shock, I realized how different this man was. He certainly was not the lion.

"My mother is a big girl, and she can make her own decisions. If you want to know what I think, it's fine with me," I said. He shook my hand, and I realized I had never shaken hands with the lion. Not ever. I liked this new guy. I was sure my mother put him up to this meeting, but you had to admire him for following through with such a request.

Mr. W was a WWII veteran and had been awarded a Purple Heart. Later, he took over his father's business as a general contractor. He built schools, churches, post offices. Just about anything he bid on, he won. He had a son who was a little younger than me and a bull of a worker. Mr. W married my mother.

It was some time later that I even began to visit them in a new house he built for her.

In 1988, while they were vacationing the Bahamas, I got appendicitis. He flew up and stayed with me while I recovered. A week following the operation, about the same time the staples were removed, I developed a deadly infection called peritonitis. I wasn't responding well, and at one point they gave me twelve to twenty-four hours to live. It was sink or swim once again! But I made it. I saw more of Mr. W in those two days than I had seen of the lion in the whole two weeks I was sick at home as a child.

Mr. W and my mom retired and moved to Florida. Vacations were hard to come by in the car business, so I'd try to visit at Christmas. I managed to get there only twice in the next twelve years. Then, in 2000, he asked me how I felt about moving to Florida. I didn't have a problem doing anything for him. He said I could be handy to have around. I think there was more to it than that because two years later, he died.

Maybe the third time is the charm. Mother had finally gotten it right. And he left too soon. I was asked to say a few words at the service. Tears streamed down my cheeks. The words weren't coming easily. Imagine, a car salesman at a loss for words. I missed my stepfather terribly.

Now, for the first time, my mother was alone. I was running a used car business and would go and see her on Sundays. Her health seemed to start fading soon after he was gone. Then she started showing signs of dementia. I assumed the everyday needs, like grocery shopping, for her.

When she died, I didn't have to hold back tears. I felt no loss. None. It didn't evoke the sorrow and tears that even the dog got. Now, I was really alone. A few years passed, and I retired. One day, right out of the blue, I realized I would need a final resting place too. I went to the local cemetery, Sea Pines, and bought a plot. Right next to me was my friend and stepfather, Mr. W, and my mother. I thought, "She'll never lose me again."

Had love found me after all?

www.ingramcontent.com/pod-product-compliance
Lightning Source LLC
LaVergne TN
LVHW011858060526
838200LV00054B/4406